Effective Project Management for Software Development

Fine Tuning Software Project Management for
Optimum Results

2nd Edition
Revised and Updated

By
Jonathan Cook

Visit the author's website for more information.

https://sites.google.com/site/jccookauthor/

Contents

Executive Summary

Software development presents a unique challenge to the project manager. Software Development is a discipline that is based more on art and craft rather than discrete engineering processes.

However, it will be rare indeed for a management team to admit to this. It is nearly universally concluded that software development is an engineering discipline subject to the normal and well defined processes of project management. It is assumed that project managers can apply all of the standard techniques of resource loading, scheduling, teams, work-breakdown-structure, etc. as they do for non software development projects.

Unfortunately, even well trained project managers, working in a well defined development method will rarely be able to track a software development project accurately and, in turn, manage the project tasks, packages, streams, etc. to a successful completion.

As is often the result, the project turns into a jumbled

mess of sub-projects partitioned out to sub teams and a plethora of blame and accusation then ensues. The project is late, over budget, out of scope and incomplete.

Introduction

Project management, as a discipline is well defined in the industrial domain. In theory it is a discipline that can be applied to virtually any type of work and in practice this is attempted. However, not all types of work are effectively managed with standardized project management tools and techniques.

There are a number of project management tools and it is not in the scope of this executive report to elaborate on the individual tools. In addition, the discipline of project management is fairly well documented and codified in various education, training and licensing practices.

The types of work that are conducive to project management techniques are those that have a well defined set of steps and disciplines that are easily duplicated across many projects. The projects can generally vary in size and scope and contain repeatable, well documented steps that cannot only be reproduced, but are also transferable to new resources and easily documented and managed within the project management framework.

This is not to say that projects that fit the project management paradigm are easy projects. Rarely is building a bridge across a gorge, creating a new skyscraper or designing and building a new airplane easy accomplishments. Rather, the steps to completing these projects are generally well defined or definable.

For example, concrete mixtures have well defined setup rates, strength calculations, pour times, etc.; steel structures have well defined engineering calculations that can be applied to architectural drawings; aeronautical lift and drag calculations can be simulated and applied to new airplane designs. And yet, even though each of these are well suited to standardized project management techniques it is not unusual for projects of these types to go well over schedule and budget.

Even more so, software development is more of an art than an engineering discipline. This is not often accepted in the management world as managers want to be able to define a project, set budgets and delivery times, manage resources and work breakdown structures, and generally have everything tied up in neat knots prior to ever writing a line of code on a new system.

Due to this lack of the acceptance of software development as art the project management techniques so lovingly applied to software projects almost always fail in their attempt to manage these projects from start to finish.

It is certainly possible to model a software project in a project management task list and Gantt chart. One can define the work breakdown structures, the resources, the time line, the budget, the scope and the expected results (generally very rosy for upper management presentation within a nice slide show). But when the rubber meets the road and the project takes flight, the project plan generally takes a nose dive to the actual evolution of the project as it progresses from initiation to (hopefully) conclusion.

This report will draw on Jonathan Cook's decades of real world experience in information technology, software development and the project management efforts that attempt to manage it. Within the framework of general project management concepts it will define the most common failures of the project management discipline as applied to software development and then provide solutions that can be used to overcome these failures.

Project Management Defined

According to the Project Management Institute:

Project management... is the application of knowledge, skills and techniques to execute projects effectively and efficiently. It's a strategic competency for organizations, enabling them to tie project results to business goals — and thus, better compete in their markets.[1]

This is a basic and strategy oriented definition and makes no reference to techniques or tools to carry out the project execution and achieve the desired results.

The tools and techniques for project management in software development and other fields is a well documented, if imperfect, collection. There are innumerable books written about, and an entire education industry revolving around, project management.

Image courtesy of Stuart Miles/FreeDigitalPhotos.net

---

[1] http://www.pmi.org/en/About-Us/About-Us-What-is-Project-Management.aspx

This Jonathan Cook executive report will not attempt to redefine project management nor attempt to change the techniques or the tools of project management. Rather it will attempt to reorient the reader in such a way that real world impediments can be overcome, resulting in world class outcomes for your projects.

Per the PMI definition, project management is the application of *knowledge, skills AND techniques*. Note that knowledge and skills make up two out of three of the listed elements. This is no accident. Techniques are worthless if applied with poor knowledge and skills.

In addition, even the best knowledge and skills may not be enough if other aspects of a project are incomplete or ill-defined.

Software as Art

Software development is NOT a process discipline. It is an art, a craft and a practice. It is emphasized in this and other Jonathan Cook executive reports that software development should not be seen as a factory floor solution, but as a creative solution.

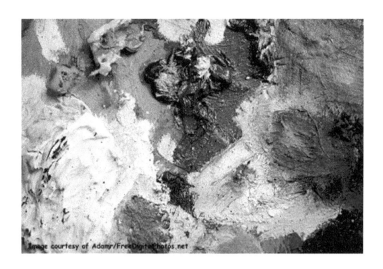

Jonathan Cook's decades of experience has taught that in order to drive quality outcomes and produce excellent results, the development process must be thought of as art and the project management process must adapt to managing an artistic process rather than an engineering process.

For example, how many times has a project fallen behind in the schedule and the first response is to drive the developers (and other people) into overdrive, demanding more work in less time, cutting vacations, working overtime, etc.? Does this work? It may produce some results for a short time, but constant pressure of this type will actually reduce results—a project manager's nightmare.

Or—new resources are hired and added to the teams with the expectation that more people will produce more results. This also tends to fail to produce the expected outcome if for no other reason then the current resources are pulled from real work in order to bring the new hires up to speed with the project. It can take months for a new resource to be truly effective in a new environment.

As such, the developer is an artists and not just a technical resource. Of course there are many arguments against considering developers as artists and Jonathan Cook does not take the perspective that software is always art (although it certainly can be) or that the developer is only an artist. Frankly, most business solutions make rather boring art displays and pure artists are often undisciplined nuts.

And many would argue that because software development is technical in nature, it must be science and engineering, not art. Thus, only strict process and organization can produce good results.

The truth lies somewhere in between and each business environment will have its own nuances that make it a unique environment. Only you can know the exact environment in which you manage projects.

Software Architecture and Engineering are not well Defined.

Software architecture[2] and software engineering[3] are, for all practical purposes, poorly defined. These poor definitions have an adverse impact on the project management process as it makes it hard for a project manager to define resources and roles if the job definitions of those resources do not necessarily align with the required tasks.

You can solve this within your own project environment by defining it internally, knowing your team regardless of titles, and assigning the appropriate work to the appropriate resources.

---

[2] http://www.sei.cmu.edu/architecture/start/glossary/moderndefs.cfm
[3] http://en.wikipedia.org/wiki/Software_Engineering_Body_of_Knowledge

Common Software Development Methods

Without repeating here research already conducted and documented in other Jonathan Cook executive reports it is highly recommended that you read the executive report **World Class Software: A New Paradigm for World Class Results.**

This report contains a detailed definition and description of many weaknesses of the commonly used Waterfall and Agile software development methods.

Each can go under various names, but the overall theme is that Waterfall is a structured development process and Agile is an adaptive process.

In a nutshell:

Image courtesy of David Castillo Dominici/FreeDigitalPhotos.net

Waterfall

A common definition of the Waterfall model might be:

The waterfall model is a sequential design process, often used in software development processes, in which progress is seen as flowing steadily downwards (like a waterfall) through the phases of Conception, Initiation, Analysis, Design, Construction, Testing, Production/Implementation, and Maintenance.[4]

---

[4] http://en.wikipedia.org/wiki/Waterfall_model

Image courtesy of Adamr/FreeDigitalPhotos.net

Agile

A common definition of the Agile model might be:

Agile software development is a group of software development methods based on iterative and incremental development, where requirements and solutions evolve through collaboration between self-organizing, cross-functional teams. It promotes adaptive planning, evolutionary development and delivery, a time-boxed iterative approach, and encourages rapid and flexible response to change. It is a conceptual framework that promotes foreseen interactions throughout the development cycle.[5]

---

[5] http://en.wikipedia.org/wiki/Agile_software_development

Each model has its pros and cons that will not be enumerated here but the details of which can be found in ***World Class Software: A New Paradigm for World Class Results.***

General Project Management Concepts (and Their Flaws and Solutions for Software Development)

It is not the intent of this executive report to teach project management nor is it intended to define or redefine the following project management terms and concepts.

Rather, it is to point out common failures in the project management processes as observed during decades of software development work in a variety of industries and organizations.

As such, this should not be used to try and train the entire universe of project management but instead be used to supplement standard project management education to help correct common mistakes as observed in the real world.

Budgeting

A list of all planned expenses (and revenues) of a project. In the real world budgets are usually defined long before the real project costs are understood and the project becomes shoe-horned into an unrealistic pre-approved budget.

Solution: Analyze your project before a budget is defined and approved. Note that the nature of Agile software development generally does not provide for extensive analysis of a project ahead of time. As such, flexible budgeting can help in an Agile environment.

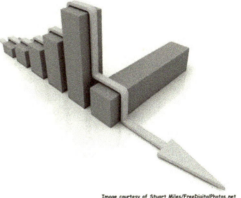

Image courtesy of Stuart Miles/FreeDigitalPhotos.net

In addition, if costs are truly considered as one of the balancing elements of a project then you must be willing to either expand a budget or cut other elements as needed to maintain the project plan.

Allocation (Human Resource)

For this definition we are considering human resources. In Jonathan Cook's experience this is one of the primary failures of project management. Resource issue are more extensively reviewed in the Jonathan Cook executive report **World Class Software: A New Paradigm for World Class Results** but in a nutshell:

Many organizations, managers and the project managers have a tendency to push for more resources in the mistaken believe that more resources will complete a project faster and better than fewer resources. Resources should be allocated to the actual requirements of the project and not to either the available resources (which may be plenty in a large organization) or a perceived tight time line.

This may sound counter-intuitive, but in the development paradigm of developer as artist and process as craft, a smaller number of artist developers can often achieve more and better quality work than a larger team of engineer developers working in a defined process.

When a project plan takes on the purely mathematical model of balancing resources, time and scope it is almost always doomed to at least significant problems if not outright failure.

Project managers also fail to properly recognize what a Full Time Equivalent resource really means.

Image courtesy of Renjith Krishnan/FreeDigitalPhotos.net

Solution: *Understand the real and practical Full Time Equivalent (FTE) resource:* An FTE is the work one person can do in one day. One day is commonly considered to be an eight hour work day. However, in practice no one works an effective full eight hours (sustainable over the long term) in one day. No matter how hard a person works, on average only about six effective hours are available in an eight hour day. Between breaks, meals, meetings, interruptions, the various crisis that pop up in every organization, vacations, sick, etc. even six hours a day is a highly effective resource.

When loading resources you should consider not work effort days (or units or other esoteric measurements), but work effort hours where six hours results in a scheduled day.

Jonathan Cook has seen project managers regularly overload resources to 200% and more. Often the project manager will not even consult the project resource reports to see the overloading. They simply throw resources at a task based on resource experience rather than availability.

If the project does not fit the fixed schedule then adjustments should be made. In no case should these adjustments create a resource overload. You can just about guarantee poor project results if resources are overloaded.

Business (Systems) Analysis

In general this means identifying the clients needs and working with the client to formulate a solution. In the drive to develop a computer based solution other elements of the solution are often overlooked. In addition, early project phase analysis often results in a simplified solution that it is not useful for the software architects, engineers and programmers. In an Agile environment this analysis often my only be a weak requirements specification.

Solution: Spend more upfront time and effort to formulate a real working analysis of the project. Even in an Agile environment the analysts on a project should at least define the main sub-components, user interfaces and system interfaces required for a project.

In addition, do not overlook the non-computer based elements of a solution. Not all things are best solved by a computer.

Change Control (and Management)

The process and management used to insure that changes are introduced in a controlled and coordinated manner. In a software development environment change control is used to (hopefully) prevent breaking things. Frankly this is an entire discipline of its own. In Jonathan Cook's experience change control is a poorly understood and executed process. One of the primary weaknesses of change control is actually due to budget management. Budgets

Image courtesy of Davd Castillo Dominici /FreeDigitalPhotos.net

rarely account for change control and when they do they rarely consider parallel change control.

Solution: Budget and plan for change control as well as the failure of change. It is not uncommon for new changes to fail. In addition, seriously consider the parallel change concept. Parallel change states that new or changing systems should be introduced in a separate parallel environment such that the parallel environment can be fully tested independent of the existing environment. When ready, the system is switched to the new parallel system and the old system is later turned off.

Communications Log

The documentation of communications between the parties involved in the execution of a project. Jonathan Cook has never observed this done in an organized, effective manner. Often email communications are the unofficial and only communication trail.

Solution: Define and enforce a communication log. This should not be used to track down and blame people, but rather as a tool to be sure all details of a project are addressed and do not fall through the cracks.

Costs and Cost Overrun

The costs (expenses) and the excess costs of a project execution. This is relatively self explanatory.

Solution: Upfront analysis; realistic, flexible budgets and resource allocations can greatly reduce costs and cost overruns. This is easier said and done, but planning and executing a project within real world constraints rather than within a fantasy world is a requirement.

Critical Path

While there is an entire school surrounding the process of the Critical Path Method (CPM), critical path in this executive report is a subset such that it represents the project pathways that must be completed and working before other pathways of the project can begin or complete.

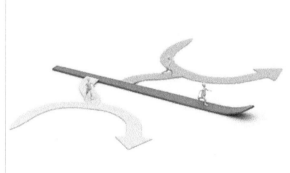

This is often overlooked or unrecognized. At its worst it is a phrase that management uses to browbeat

Image courtesy of Renjith Krishan/FreeDigitalPhotos.net

resources into working harder and faster on what management determines is important at the time.

Solution: Proper upfront analysis can determine the true critical paths of a project. Appropriate focus and resources can then be applied.

Dependency

Simply put it is the dependency one project task or path has on another task or path within a project. Task dependency can be fairly obvious within a small time frame that is tracked accurately. Broader dependencies can be harder to track.

Similar to Critical Path, the dependencies are often overlooked or just tied together based on nearby tasks in the task list.

Solution: Proper upfront analysis can determine the true dependencies of a project. Dependencies must be looked at on both a narrow and broad scale basis and not just within a range of tasks. Appropriate focus and resources can then be applied.

Duration

How long it takes to complete a project element. This is heavily dependent on good estimation and execution. Duration becomes more difficult to estimate and track if the development environment is a flexible Agile process while the Project Management environment is a fixed Waterfall process.

Solution: The development process and the project management process should be aligned. If not then a determined emphasis on good upfront analysis can better determine the project element durations.

Deliverable

A tangible result delivered as agreed. The main failure with deliverables, as observed by Jonathan Cook, is poorly defined deliverables such that no one really understands what and when a deliverable is actually delivered.

Solution: Clearly define your deliverables and what constitutes a completed deliverable. Within an Agile environment this may be referred to as "*Done*".

Estimation

Making accurate estimates. Usually referring to time, costs, resources and completion schedules. Proper estimating is a major failure in the project management field, especially in software development projects. This is mainly due to the fact that it is difficult to estimate the resources and duration of tasks and deliverables that are, for all practical purposes, invention. Estimating software is like estimating invention. Unless you can reuse all of the code from a previous project (thus probably not developing anything new) you are going to need to create new code and you are essentially inventing new software.

Experienced developers can make reasonable estimates for much of a software development project because they have a good knowledge base of how to complete many of the elements used in most software (user interfaces, database actions, etc.). However, it is the unique requirements that are more difficult to estimate and that are prone to estimation failure.

Solution: Most projects will base their estimates on

the advise of these experienced resources. Project managers should listen to the resources and use their estimates. If the project does not fit the fixed schedule then adjustments should be made. In no case should these adjustments create a resource overload. You can guarantee poor project results if estimates are ignored and resources are overloaded.

Goals

Essentially, what the project and its deliverables are trying to accomplish. Goals are often nebulous and ill-defined. In addition, it is hard to train users, subject matter experts and analysts on goal definition and goal establishment for a  project as goals are very esoteric in nature.

Poorly defined goals often take on the characteristics of wishes or desires. Things such as *improve the user experience* or *reduce downtime* sound good, but have very little real definition and nothing measurable.

Solution: Define goals that are tangible and measurable. Define when a goal is complete. Match goals to project deliverables and measurable results.

Iteration

(Increment(al), sprint, iteration, etc.): A cyclical, repeatable time duration in which a defined set of deliverable outcomes is worked upon. Generally used within an Agile development method framework.

Within an iteration the tasks are defined and performed to meet the deliverables. Anything that is not accomplished is pushed out to a later iteration.

In theory, at the end of an iteration, production ready software is complete and ready for deployment. However, in practice iterations often miss their deliverables. As a project moves forward more and more items are deferred, time is consumed and the project falls behind.

Solution: Good estimation is key to good iteration planning. In addition, iterations should be of a reasonable length of time to account for resource loading and availability. If an iteration is two short (one to two weeks) resources may have too little time to actually accomplish anything meaningful (an FTE resource has only 30 effective hours per week).

Furthermore, you must plan for critical paths that have a duration greater than an iteration. This most often occurs in large projects in which extended teams need to complete long term deliverables upon which other teams are dependent to complete their deliverables (system interfaces are a common example).

If production ready is in the deliverable definition, then the iteration must account for full unit testing, QA testing and bug fixes.

Project Manager

The professional that handles the management of a project. This may sound obvious, but *professional* is the operative word. Too often a person is selected to be a project manager because they have some experience with the available project management tool and can enter the tasks. However, they may have little other project management experience. **Solution**: Be sure your managers are well trained in project management.

Project Stakeholders

The sponsors and others who have *skin in the game* of a project. These are the managers procuring the budgets, the users (represented by business subject matter experts [SMEs] or super-users) and others impacted by the outcome of the project. The stakeholders can be a vast group, but in general they are limited to those providing the money and those immediately consuming the results.

The main failure of the stakeholders is not enough involvement in the project process. This most often occurs because the stakeholders are ignored by the project team once the requirements are defined and budgets approved. The stakeholders will also often pull away from project involvement assuming that the project team has everything under control.

Solution: Both sides need to stay involved and communication needs to be immediate and complete. Do not hide things and do not assume things.

Risk (Risk Management)

This is a management specialty of its own and volumes of material is available for review on the subject. Suffice it to say that risk is rarely well managed in the real world.

This is most often due to fear, ignorance or willful neglect. Team members, managers and project managers may be afraid to expose risk in the fear of looking bad to supervisors and others on the team. Or risk may simply be overlooked. Worst of all is willful neglect (usually by upper management) to ignore a risk and sweep it under the carpet in hopes that it will work out somehow.

Solution: Stay on top of risk. Do not ignore it. Expose it early and address it. Project managers need to hunt for risk and vigorously pursue it to resolution.

Scope (and Scope Creep)

This is essentially the sum total of all aspects of a project. To the client this usually means the feature set of a project. To the project team it usually means all of the tasks and deliverables as well as the feature set to be delivered. Scope creep means the slow (and painful) expansion of the scope by additional client requests for more features.

Scope and Scope Creep failure most often occur due to poor requirements and poor communications. In addition, scope creep is magnified by the project management teams inability to say NO to the client. This increases work, but not time or resources/budgets.

Solution: Well defined requirements and good communications are a must for any development method. In addition, clients have to be told, and have to accept, that additional requests cannot be added without impact to the project.

The Agile development method attempts to address the scope issue by injecting flexibility into the development process. In theory, as the client works closely with the project team, changes become an accepted part of the process. In reality, the Agile method can be just as susceptible to scope issues since the cause of the issues don't automatically resolve just because the Agile method is invoked. Changes still create estimate revisions and delays, and poor communications still cause problems.

Work Breakdown Structure (WBS)

A grouping of the project's discrete work elements to help organize and define the total work of a project. WBS by itself is just a tool. Failure can occur if the Agile development method is used and the WBS is not aligned with the project's Agile task and iteration planning. Essentially the project manager is expecting progress as mapped in the WBS and the development team is making progress as mapped by the tasks and iterations in play/flight. If the too are not aligned then expectations clash. This is exaggerated when extended teams follow different development methods and/or when using multiple tools to manage a project (For example, the project manager may be using a standard project management system and the Agile team may be using a task and iteration management tool that is better at tracking small tasks, resources and backlogs rather than project items and resource dependencies.).

Solution: Find a common, coordinated tool set to manage a project and in the case of an Agile project, work to align the project plan with the iteration plan.

Conclusion

This executive report has provided the reader with the opinion of Jonathan Cook based on decades of experience in the field of Information Technology.

It provides insights and advice that in the opinion of Jonathan Cook will help you fine tune your processes by introducing elements and ideas often overlooked in the standard professional texts and consulting services.

After reading this text it is hoped that you will be able to find new ways to enhance your project management techniques and improve your results.

www.ingramcontent.com/pod-product-compliance
Lightning Source LLC
Chambersburg PA
CBHW051124050326
40690CB00006B/801